the Story of Christmas for Children

CATHARINE BRANDT

AUGSBURG PUBLISHING HOUSE • MINNEAPOLIS, MINNESOTA

THE STORY OF CHRISTMAS FOR CHILDREN
Copyright © 1974 Augsburg Publishing House
Library of Congress Catalog Card No. 74-79366
International Standard Book No. 0-8066-1426-9

All rights reserved

Manufactured in the United States of America

the story of christmas for children

The Story of Christmas

This is the story of two people who lived almost two thousand years ago in the little town of Nazareth far across the ocean. They might have lived and died in Nazareth, and nobody except their family and friends would ever have heard of them.

But one day something happened that made them famous in the whole world.

Mary was a gentle young woman who loved God and obeyed Him. Her name means "loved of God." She was getting ready to marry Joseph, a kind and strong man, a carpenter. They were poor people and worked hard every day.

Mary sewed clothing and gathered jugs and bowls for her new home. Joseph chopped down a sycamore tree and sawed beams and posts. He used them to build a little house of wood and sun-baked clay for them to live in. It had only one room.

Life was not very happy for the people in Nazareth. Their ruler was Caesar Augustus, the Roman emperor, who ruled over many lands. He was cruel to God's people, and they feared him. But they prayed to God. They knew God loved them. They often met in a place called the synagogue to hear someone read from the Word of God.

When Mary went to the synagogue, she could not walk in the center door with Joseph. She had to go around to the side with the other women and children and climb stone steps on the outside to a balcony. There Mary could peek over the edge and listen to the leader down below reading from the Word of God.

God had promised to send them a king, a Savior who would deliver His people from their enemies. Mary heard the men talk about God's love. She heard them pray that God would send the Savior soon.

Mary listened carefully. She nodded her head with the others. Everyone, men and women, boys and girls, sang together. As Mary sang she felt good. She thought, "God will keep His promise. He will send a Savior."

The Angel Visits Mary

God had a plan. His plan was to send His own Son as a tiny baby to show all people how much He loved them. God was the Father, but a baby needs a family to care for it.

One day God sent His angel Gabriel to tell Mary that He had chosen her to be the mother of His Son. At first Mary was afraid of the bright light and the angel who had come like the clap of hands. Mary covered her eyes and trembled. Nothing like this had ever happened to her before.

"Mary, the Lord is with you," said the angel.

What could the angel mean?

"Do not be afraid, Mary," the angel said. "You will have a son, and you will call Him Jesus. He will be great and will be called Son of the Most High. He will be king forever."

At first Mary was so surprised she couldn't talk. But she loved God and wanted to obey Him.

Mary said, "I am the Lord's servant. I am ready to do whatever He wants."

Then the angel left her.

Afterwards Mary made up a beautiful song that begins, "My soul magnifies the Lord." Mary wanted to praise God because He had chosen her to be the mother of the long-promised Savior, the baby she would call Jesus.

God sent an angel to tell Joseph too. "Mary's baby is from God," the angel said. "You shall give Him the name Jesus for He shall save His people from their sins."

Joseph believed the words of the angel, and Mary and Joseph were married. They lived in the little house Joseph had built. With his hammer and nails he made a bench for Mary to sit on and a bed for the baby. Close by their house were olive trees, and in the distance Mary and Joseph could see fields where sheep grazed. Joseph often thought about what the angel had told him. He believed that Mary's baby would be the Savior.

God made sure that Jesus would have a loving mother. And He made sure that the child would have a kind and good father.

The Emperor's Command

One day iron wheels of a Roman chariot and horses' hooves pounded through the dusty streets of the quiet little town of Nazareth. Boys and girls ran into the house to hide. The men jumped out of the way of the charging horses. When the chariot stopped on the main street, the men ran close to hear what the messengers had to say.

A Roman soldier jumped out of the chariot. He unrolled an announcement from Caesar Augustus and began to read in a loud voice. "Hear the Emperor's command. Everyone must return to his own town to have his name written in a book and be counted."

Joseph and Mary would have to go to Bethlehem. Joseph worried about the journey to Bethlehem, almost eighty miles away.

"It is nearly time for the baby to be born," he thought. But when Caesar Augustus said, "Go," people went, even if it was hard for them.

While Joseph got their little donkey ready for the journey, Mary filled a jug of water. She took a clay lamp and some oil. She packed olives and figs and a thick loaf of bread. She folded the wrapping blankets for the new baby and took them too. Joseph put it all into the basket tied on the side of the donkey.

Mary brought out their cloaks to keep them warm. A cloak was full and long, made of sheep's wool, spun and woven. A traveler could spread it on the ground for a bed and cover himself with it.

Joseph helped Mary up on the donkey. The donkey turned its head and blinked, as if to say, "I'll carry you safely." Mary patted the animal's furry neck. Joseph took the bridle, and they started out for Bethlehem.

Mile after mile Joseph led the little donkey. Mary often sang as she rode along. Now and then they stopped so Mary could rest. At night they slept, wrapped in their warm cloaks. Stars stretched across the dark sky. One star looked larger and brighter than all the others.

When they could see the town of Bethlehem not far away, Joseph stopped on a hill. He thought again about the words of the angel that Mary's baby would be the Savior. It was almost time for the baby to be born.

God Keeps His Promise

Late in the day they came to Bethlehem. The rough stone streets were crowded with people and animals. Dogs barked as they ran alongside the donkey. Men were buying and selling food and bracelets and brightly colored cloth. Shouting in the street, they shoved and pushed each other. Joseph wanted to find a quiet place for Mary away from the noisy crowd.

He stopped at the inn first. But the innkeeper shouted, "No room. No room. Move on."

Then the innkeeper saw Mary. He called a boy and handed him a light, a thick branch of a sycamore tree, wet with oil and set afire.

"Take them to the stable in the cave behind the inn," he said. "Tomorrow we will look for a better place."

Carefully Joseph followed the boy with the light. He led the donkey carrying Mary along the steep path behind the inn to the stable-cave. Joseph helped Mary down and found a place for her in the clean straw of the cave. He lighted the lamp Mary had brought from home and put it in a safe place.

"I'll be back as soon as I take care of the donkey," he said.

Joseph tied up the animal and fed it. "Let me look at your feet," he said to the donkey. "You may have picked up a sharp stone that cut you."

Joseph stroked the donkey. "Here's a chunk of honeycomb because you carried Mary safely on the long jour-

ney. You were not a bit stubborn." Then Joseph washed the dust from his own feet.

In the stable the oxen crunched their hay. The heat of their bodies warmed the cool air of the cave. The sheep and goats blinked their eyes at the light from Mary's lamp. In a corner doves fluttered their wings.

One by one the animals in the stable quieted down. The doves sat very still. The noisy crowd at the inn had gone to sleep. Even the dogs had stopped barking. Outside the sky was very bright.

Here, in the quiet stable, God kept His promise. Mary gave birth to her son and wrapped Him in swaddling clothes, narrow strips of cloth mothers used for tiny babies. She held Him in her arms a long time. Joseph put clean straw in one of the feeding bins. Mary stretched a little blanket over the straw and laid the baby on it.

"This is not a good bed," she told Joseph. "When we go back home to Nazareth, I'll put Him in the little bed you made."

Then they all slept—the baby Jesus, Mary, Joseph, and the friendly animals.

Shepherds Hear the Good News

On the hills outside Bethlehem that night shepherds were watching their flocks. They took turns sleeping so someone could protect the sheep from wild animals. The shepherds who stayed awake often played tunes on their reed flutes.

All at once a bright light blazed a path in the dark sky from heaven to

earth. The shepherds at first covered their eyes with their hands. When they looked around, they saw an angel of the Lord. They were afraid and tried to get away from the light. Nothing so sudden and bright had ever happened to them before. Keeping an eye on the angel, they nudged the sleeping shepherds with their feet.

"Wake up," they whispered.

The angel said, "Do not be afraid. I bring you good news of a great joy which will come to all the people; for to you is born this day in the city of David a Savior, who is Christ the Lord. And this will be a sign to you: you will find a baby wrapped in swaddling clothes and lying in a manger."

Suddenly the sky was filled with light and angels all singing, "Glory to God in the highest, and on earth peace, good will toward men." After the sounds of the sky-song faded away, the angel left the shepherds.

"What does it mean? Why did the angel tell us about the wonderful birth? What shall we do?" The shepherds were full of questions.

One said, "Let us go to Bethlehem and see what the angel has told us." One old man and some young boys stayed behind to watch the sheep, while the shepherds ran down the steep hills toward Bethlehem.

They soon found the stable behind the inn, and inside they saw the baby on His bed of hay, with Mary and Joseph nearby. One by one the shepherds came close to see the new baby. They thanked God for sending this child to be the Savior, for they believed the words of the angel.

Soon the shepherds walked out of the stable and into the early morning. They were excited and talked to

one another about the angel and the baby. People poked their heads out of doors to see what all the noise was about. The shepherds told the news to everyone they saw.

"Christ the Savior is born," they shouted.

"Back there in the stable behind the inn."

"The angel told us while we were watching our sheep."

"Go and see for yourselves."

Mary never forgot the shepherds' visit. She remembered everything the angel had told her and prayed to God for her little boy. What did it all mean? What would her baby be like when He grew up?

Mary and Joseph named their baby Jesus as the angel had said. When Jesus was forty days old it was time for them to take Him to the great temple in Jerusalem to be blessed. They would present Him to God, as written in God's Word, and bring a gift of two young pigeons. The gift would show their thanks for the baby Jesus.

Joseph untied their donkey and helped Mary up on it. Then he handed her the baby and started on the six-mile trip to the big city of Jerusalem. When they reached the city, they could see the white and gold temple shining in the sun. They had never seen anything so beautiful.

Just as Mary and Joseph brought Jesus into the temple, an old man stopped them.

"I am Simeon," he said. Then he took Jesus from Mary and held Him carefully in his arms. "God's Holy Spirit told me that before I die, I would see the Savior. This morning the Spirit told me to come to the temple." Then he thanked God.

Mary and Joseph were too surprised to speak. They stood quietly while Simeon blessed them.

The Star and the Wise Men

When Mary and Joseph returned from Jerusalem, they saw a bright light, like a big star, in the sky at night. It seemed to shine right down on the house where they were.

One evening they heard the thud of camels' feet outside. When Mary looked out, she saw that the camels had already bent their knees to the ground so the riders could get off. The men looked up at the sky. The large star was shining brightly over the house.

"This is the place," one of the strangers said.

"We have studied the skies and have looked for the great king a long time," they told Joseph. "Now we know He has been born. We saw His star in the East and followed it. We crossed mountains and deserts in cold weather, cold enough to snow. We want to worship the new king."

Joseph was surprised that the wise men from so far away knew about Jesus.

"First we went to Jerusalem," one of the wise men said. "We asked King Herod where to find the new-born king. His helpers told him that the new king had been born in Bethlehem. Herod told us to keep looking for the king and to let him know when we found Him."

When the wise men saw the child and Mary His mother, they knelt down and worshiped Him. Then they opened their bags and gave Him gold, frankincense, and myrrh (ointment and perfume that smelled like candles burning). Only very rich men could give such presents.

"In the morning we will return to Herod to tell him where the new king is," they told Joseph.

But in the night God sent an angel in a dream to warn them.

"Don't go back to Herod," the angel said. "He is a wicked king and wants to harm the young child."

The wise men believed the angel, and they took a different road back to their homes in the East.

Joseph Has a Dream

That very night an angel said to Joseph, "Get up right now. Take the child and His mother and run for your lives to Egypt. Stay there until I tell you to come back. Herod is looking for the child to kill Him."

Joseph threw back the covers, awakened Mary, and hurried to get the donkey ready for their escape. Mary put food and extra clothing on a blanket. She added the money and gifts the wise men had left and then tied it all up in a bundle to take with them. In the dark of night Joseph led the donkey carrying Mary and the child as they started their long trip to Egypt.

Even as they ran away from danger, wicked King Herod showed what he really wanted to do.

"Where are the wise men?" he shouted. "I ordered them to come back and tell me where the new king is. They have not done it. They have tricked me."

Herod was in a furious rage, and he was afraid that this new king would take his place, so he commanded that all little boys in Bethlehem two years old and younger should be killed.

But God took care of the baby Jesus. He sent an angel to tell Joseph what to do, and Joseph obeyed.

The family did not stay long in Egypt. The wicked Herod soon died. Again God sent an angel to Joseph.

"Take the young child and His mother and go back to your own country," the angel said. "It is now safe for you to go."

Joseph brought Mary and Jesus to their home in Nazareth. The boy slept in the bed Joseph had made. Jesus grew like any other boy. Mary and Joseph watched Him crawl and walk and run. Joseph showed Him how to work with tools and be a good carpenter. Jesus loved Mary and Joseph.

On that special night we call Christmas God gave the world His Son, born as a baby, because He wanted us to understand how much He loves us.

The baby grew to be a man. He was a great and wise teacher. He loved God and helped all people. He gave His life to be the Savior of the whole world. One day He said, "For God so loved the world that He gave His only Son, that whoever believes in Him should not perish but have eternal life."